J. F. MACAIGNE - P. BASTIER
–
Translated from french by
AARON JANOFSKY

Wandering through
ALSACE

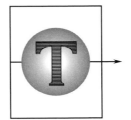

ALSACE is a magical land; spirits and dwarves rub shoulders daily with tourists in an ageless region strangely resembling those of the fairy tale books of our childhood. Yet the most modern enterprises, operating in towns as well as in the heart of the countryside, bring tradition and history face to face with nascent twenty-first century technology. Without a doubt Alsace is an enchanted land. What better proof than the storks, which for so many years have delivered babies into Alsatian chimneys, who pass their summer vacation here? In fact, recently these magnificent birds have decided to stay year round.

Before embarking on our exploration of the paths and byways of Alsace, let us glance at the history of this region whose past has been tied to that of France since the end of the Thirty Years War.

Bordered to the east by the Rhine river, which separates Alsace from Germany, and to the west by the Vosges Mountains, this ancient swampy plain was slowly settled by men who brought with them agriculture, notably the grapevine, a subject to which we will return...

The Celts, first inhabitants of the region, were soon pushed out by the Romans who occupied Alsace as a buffer against invasion from the east. The Pax Romana reigned for many years, almost until the Holy Roman Empire annexed the land in the tenth century. Commerce developed with prosperity, and ten towns liberated themselves from feudal domination and established the Décapole, a federation of free cities. The spirit of independence of the federation's inhabitants survives today as one may see from a visit to Wissembourg or Colmar. After the Treaty of Westphalia (1648), at the end of the Thirty Years War, Alsace became French. For only a few years, after being annexed by the Second Reich in 1870 and until being liberated by French troops in 1918, has Alsace been German.

Land of tolerance, where Catholics and Protestants sometimes share the same church steeple, Alsace cultivates her traditions, her differences, and her joie de vivre. Let us begin our journey by saying hello to the storks...

THE STORKS, living symbols of Alsace and flying legends dear to the hearts of all Alsatians, began to decline in number in the 1970s, to the point of becoming curiosities, rarities even! The birds were migrating to Africa but returning only in very small numbers. Hunted and slain by both local peoples and Europeans on safari, it became urgent at a time when nature's balance was upset to remedy the situation.

It is this task that M. RENAUD has accepted in his Center for the Reintroduction of the Storks in Hunawihr: "Because those birds that migrate in the fall do not return to their nests in the springtime, we must encourage them not to leave." It was a matter, then, of suppressing the migratory instincts of these birds. Since 1976 one hundred and fifty to two hundred storks have lived and reproduced in complete liberty in this nature reserve. Because the Center provides food and heated nesting areas against the difficult Alsatian winter, the reproduction rate has attained a level never before seen in wild storks. Every

A little tenderness...
A space of freedom for the storks

Between the otter and the sea-lion, it is a festival of trickery. A show not to be missed for any reason! Visitors may also view more than twenty types of fish that live in the region's streams and lakes in the Center's cold water aquarium gallery.

year thirty to fifty young storks are born to re-populate the chimneys and church towers of Alsace. The majority of those storks found in Ribeauvillé, Sélestat, or Ostheim come from the Center.

In Hunawihr one may, of course, view the storks but also admire as well herons and some of the most beautiful ducks in the world. Also to be seen is an aquatic show unique in Europe: a 250,000 liter aquarium in which frolic an otter, a sea-lion, cormorants, and penguins. The spectacle is a joyous but unusual sight. The roly-poly and out-going penguins literally fly through the water at more than fifty kilometers per hour. The cormorants, real underwater missiles, juggle with eels before swallowing them.

Getting out from the pool...
Dessert for the otter
The flight of the penguin underwater

In Alsace, no festival without a band
Dresses from Geispolsheim / Costumes from Meistratzheim

An almost uncountable number of traditional Alsatian costumes exist, most of which unfortunately never leave the closet except during festivals or tourist events. Each region, each village possesses its own costume, differing from those of neighboring areas according to geographical location, economic factors, and, of course, fashion. One of the most well-known accessories, the schlupfkapp, a bonnet with a big black bow, became fashionable after the Germans occupied Alsace in 1870. Along with the blue, white, and red cocarde badge, Alsatian women wore the schlupfkapp to show their attachment to France. The drawings of the Alsatian artist Hansi helped popularize the image of men wearing red vests under black coats and of women favoring red skirts. If you attend one of the many Alsatian folklore festivals, you will be able to see for yourself, first-hand, the wide variety of dress that really exists.

Tradition of the costumes
Tradition of the table

WISSEMBOURG, GATEWAY TO FRANCE

One day good King Dagobert presented lands to an abbey situated on the sight of present-day Wissembourg. This abbey, founded by Saint Firmin, would at the beginning of the Middle Ages exert its influence throughout all of Europe and give birth to a village mentioned for the first time in a police regulation of 1265. The town fortified itself, joined the Décapole, and became the arena for many a combat. Part of the monastery wall dating from the eleventh century, watched over by the "Schartenturm" to the west of the town, exists today.

In 1720 the king of Poland Stanislas Leszcynski settled with his daughter Marie into a house, later converted into a hospital, in the center of town. It was here that the Duc d'Antin came in 1725 to ask the hand of Marie in the name of Louis XV. Louis was fifteen, Marie twenty-two.

In the heart of Wissembourg rises Saint-Pierre and Saint-Paul, the abbey church of the old monastery. After the cathedral of Strasbourg, Saint-Pierre and Saint-Paul is the largest Gothic church in Alsace. Furthermore, the church has retained from its Romanesque origins its square tower. The church's cloister is generally considered to be the most beautiful to be found in the valley of the Rhine.

The Schlupf and the Lauter river   *Roofs of Wissembourg / detail of a half-timbered house*
The roof of the "Salt House"

Walking through the narrow streets of the "Schlupf" and strolling along the banks of the Lauter, one discovers the "Salt House", the first town hospital which was subsequently transformed into a storeroom for salt and then in the seventeenth century into a slaughterhouse. Farther along, the house of "l'Ami Fritz", which served as the location for the film, exhibits a typical Alsatian bay window and entry dating from 1550. To be admired also is the famous "Maison Vogelsberger" whose owner Colonel Vogelsberger was decapitated in 1548 on orders from Charles Quint for having attended the coronation in Reims of Henry II.

A must for admirers of Bartholdi, creator of the Statue of Liberty and the Lion of Belfort, is a visit to "l'Ancienne Couronne", an inn until 1603 and then home to the family of the famous sculptor.

Finally, one must not leave Wissembourg without having seen the Westercamp Museum where archives, seals, charters, engravings, arms, uniforms, and costumes revive the turbulent history of this charming town, all in a construction dating from 1591.

The house of "L'Ami Fritz"
The cloister of the abbey church Saint-Pierre-et-Saint-Paul

HAGUENAU

The troops of Louis XIV razed the fortifications and the castle of Haguenau in 1677 in order to erase a fabulous past, that of the Hohenstaufen. This great family reigned over an empire stretching from the North Sea to Sicily. Frederick II Barbarossa was without a doubt the most famous member of this dynasty. The castle's model at the history museum reflects the importance of the fortress as well as the extraordinary construction of the chapel, composed of three superimposed naves, the last of which housed the empire's treasure. It was here, in fact, that Charlemagne's sceptre, sword, coat, and crown were kept, along with holy relics including a nail from Christ's cross, a thorn from his crown, and the spear of Longinus used to pierce Jesus' flank.

The town lived memorable moments like the judging of Richard the Lionhearted by the Emperor Henry VII in 1193, a scene represented in the stained glass windows of the town museum. The museum also houses a fabulous collection of objects from the Mesolithic, Neolithic, and Bronze Ages.

Only the Tower of the Horsemen and the Tower of the Fishermen remain of the twelfth century wall, but the Church of Saint Georges, also built during the eleven hundreds, still possesses the lattice work of the transept, its polygonal apses, and the two oldest church bells in Alsace (1268).

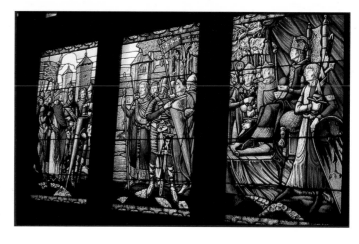

Saint-Georges church *The Town Hall astronomical clock*
The Tower of the Fishermen
The "Richard the Lionhearted" stained glass window, at the Historical Museum

SESSENHEIM,

near Haguenau, was witness to Goethe's love for Frédérique Brion, daughter of the town's pastor, whom the German writer met while studying in Strasbourg. At the "Au Boeuf" Inn the letters and portraits of the young lovers are piously preserved.

Nearby, between Haguenau, Sessenheim, and Strasbourg, spreads a large part of Alsace's tobacco fields. Interested parties may visit tobacco farms and factories.

In the recess of a door
A tobacco dryer in Pfulgriesheim
The half timbered houses in Bouxwiller

SAVERNE

Originally a Roman garrison founded to guard the passage between the two regions of Lorraine and Alsace, Saverne was a way station around which flourished country inns, hence the name Tres Tabernae (Three Taverns) which became Saverne. The town kept its military and commercial character, despite being dominated by the bishops of Metz, then by the dukes of Alsace, and finally by the bishops of Strasbourg in the 13th century. In 1525 "les Rustauds", or the members of a peasant revolt, took control of the town, plundering and setting fire to its patrician houses. The episode ended with the massacre of the peasants by troops of the Duke Antoine de Lorraine despite the latters orders for clemency.

The bishops of Strasbourg established their administrative center and residence in Saverne, far from their own city's agitation and the Reformation. These bishops built the town palace which over the centuries became known as the "Palais des Rohan". Destroyed by fire, the episcopal dwelling of the seventeenth century was rebuilt and enlarged by Armand-Gaston de Rohan-Soubise. The destruction of this second

The Rohan palace
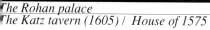
The Katz tavern (1605) / House of 1575

structure in 1779, again by fire, gave Louis-René de Rohan-Guémené the occasion to rebuild, with the help of the architect Nicolas Salins de Montfort, an even more ostentatious lodging. The so-called "Queen's necklace" scandal prevented completion of work. The palace was finally finished when Napoleon transformed it into a residence for the widows of civil servants. One should not leave the town and its region without seeing "Prince Charles' Leap" located in the Saverne mountain pass. During a hunting outing in 1774 Duke Charles of Lorraine miscalculated a jump on his horse and found himself and his mount falling some twenty meters. The impact was so great that the horse, which limped back to Saverne, left imprints of its iron shoes in the rock. In the Vosges Mountains we find similar marks resembling horseshoes. The Celts considered horses as symbols of the sun, and Sleipnir, the God Odin's mount, limped in winter and regained his strength in the summer. This tale illustrates how the existence of a solar cult with its pagan beliefs became a local legend.

A few miles farther and dominated from a distance by the castles of Haut Barr and Grand Geroldseck, the town of Marmoutier shelters one of the most beautiful Alsatian Romanesque churches. The abbey building whose red clay facade can be dated to about 1150 reminds us of the sixth century abbey once found in the same location that gave its name to the village. Abbot Maur having introduced the strict rule of Saint Benoit to the area, the faithful named the monastery Mauri Monasterium which soon became Marmoutier.

The Saint-Etienne abbey church in Marmoutier
The Lichtenberg castle   *The "Petite-Pierre" castle*

THE REGIONAL PARK OF THE NORTH VOSGES MOUNTAINS spreads over 120,000 hectares from Saverne to the German border and from the Sarre Union to Wissembourg. The park's administrative headquarters, based in Petite Pierre Castle, are deep in the heart of the forest on the road linking the Lorraine region with the Alsace plain. Built in the twelfth century, the castle was occupied in succession by Germans, Swedes, and the French during the Thirty Years War. In 1680 under Louis XIV France definitively annexed the castle which Vauban rebuilt adding military barracks.

Several miles from La Petite Pierre Castle Saint-Jean-de-Saverne offers those interested in Romanesque art the Chapel of Saint-Michel as well as the ancient church of a Benedictine abbey.

The forest
The Hanau pond / An encounter always possible..

Dominated by the ruins of Herenstein Castle, Neuwiller-les-Saverne is the perfect rest stop with its picturesque Saint-Pierre-and-Saint Paul Church and its two superimposed chapels (XI century) before arriving at Ingwiller, famous for its onion-shaped domed synagogue. A few steps down the road rises the Stone of the Twelve Apostles, sculpted in the eighteenth century, and the medieval castle of Lichtenberg whose keep, constructed in the twelve hundreds, towers above the village below.

The park offers many other destinations like the castles of Fleckenstein, Wassembourg, Hohenbourg or the Hanau Pond and the Eschwiller Windmill, the perfect place for those who

A fox, which looks as surprised as you to be here... / A strange rock, carved by the wind Erbsenfelds, nearby Hanau pond

love the water and the sun to pass a beautiful summer day. However, the unique charm of the park really derives from the many hiking paths through woods and across fields, among wild animals, and amidst an ever changing forest. Tourists will find maps, addresses, information and helpful hints at the park headquarters in the Petite Pierre Castle.

The abundance of small museums where one can see craftsmen making wooden shoes, creating glassware and fine crystal makes the park all the more attractive. Among other park

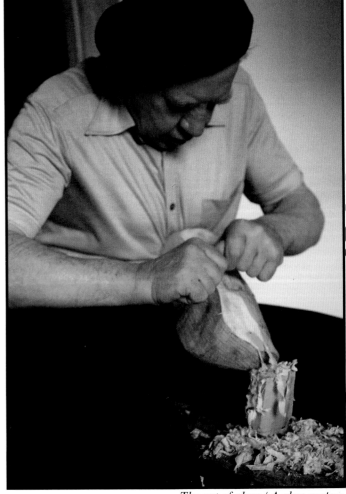

The art of glass / A clog-maker

museums are those of the image, of Alsatian traditions, and of ancient crafts. In Bouxwiller at the Hanau Museum one finds an impressive collection of traditional polychrome furniture, country pewter, kitchen utensils, and earthenware from the Lorraine. At the glass and crystal house in Meisenthal where Gallé practiced his art, one can view superb exhibits by craftsmen who work with these materials. In Offwiller, at the Village House, one imagines the life of last century's peasants. On the Sunday that follows Mardi Gras be sure not to miss the *schieweschlawe*, a custom which has the town's inhabitants throwing red hot plates from the top of the hill.

Museum of Bouxwiller
Museum of Phalsbourg

STRASBOURG

Ladies first! A visit to Strasbourg begins imperatively with a visit to Notre Dame, one of the most beautiful cathedrals of the world. The history of the city can be read in the stones and walls of this jewel of a cathedral.

Begun in 1015 in the Romanesque style, the original basilica was built on the site of an ancient Roman temple dedicated to Hercules. In 1145 Saint Bernard came here to celebrate mass. Several years later, however, fire ravaged the building.

Work on today's cathedral began in 1176 with the construction, in the pink sandstone of the Vosges Mountains, of part of the eastern side of the building. The art and architecture of the Ile de France, or the region surrounding Paris, clearly influenced the master builder. This same master was also to erect the famous Pillar of Angels. Between 1240 and 1275 the nave was built. From 1277 on, Master Erwin de Steinbach, then his son Jean, and finally Master Gerlach constructed the facade in the most pure Gothic style. The towers on either side of the facade were finished in 1365, and around 1370 Michael de Fribourg joined them by constructing a belfry above the rose window. In 1399 Ulrich von Ensingen raised the octagonal north tower on which Johannes Hültz, an architect from Cologne, erected the spire which looms 142 meters above street level.

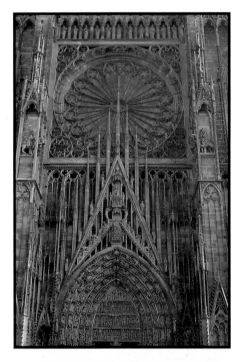

Notre Dame has had a turbulent history since. In the sixteenth century during the

Notre-Dame of Strasbourg | *The foolish virgins*
The central Portal and the rose-window
The Tympanum

- 21 -

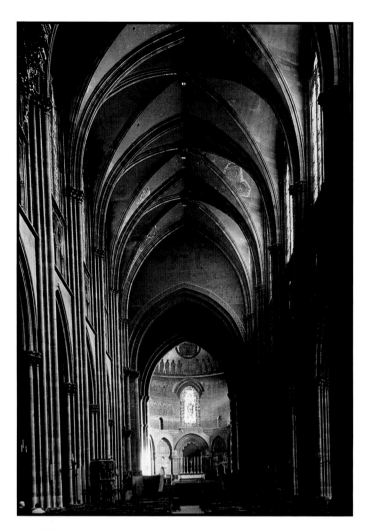

Reformation statues were removed and altars destroyed. During the French Revolution 230 figures were smashed, and the cathedral survived only because of the astonishing idea of a local citizen who suggested capping the spire with a gigantic red Phrygian bonnet, the typical revolutionary headdress. In 1903 Johan Knauth, Notre Dame's master architect at the time, succeeded in saving the western tower that had threatened to collapse. Finally, in 1944 American bombs fell on the cathedral, notably on the tower capping the transept crossing. To appreciate fully Notre Dame as well as to contemplate it's original statues, one must pay a visit to the Œuvre Notre-Dame House across the square. Administered by the town since 1286, the museum is the perfect place to feel the ancient presence of stonemasons and craftsmen. One may also relive the construction of the cathedral and perhaps even meet one of the masters who have since the Middle Ages kept the cathedral a living monument by continually restoring, protecting, and loving it. Among the interesting elements making up Notre Dame is the astronomical clock, the mechanics of which were devised by the Strasbourgeois Jean-Baptiste Schwilgué, which keeps time but is always late by a half hour. The chimes for noon sound at 12:30, and at this moment out of the clock case appear the twelve apostles who bow in front of the statue of Jesus while a mechanical rooster beats its wings and sings out three times. Aside from this show, the figure representing death sounds every hour and those of the four ages of life every quarter of an hour.

The nave
The astronomical clock / The Pillar of Angels

Few cities have the charms of Strasbourg. At the heart of Europe, at the gateway between France and Germany, the city is a meeting place for peoples from the east, the south, and the west.

From neolithic times man has inhabited the region. The Triboques, a Gaullic tribe of fishermen, settled the area and were followed by the Romans who were greatly interested in this natural crossroads of river and land routes. Argentoratum, the city's first name, was originally founded as a military camp surrounding the old Gaullic village which was ideally situated to protect from the barbarians to the east. Germanic tribes and the Huns devastated the town which the Franks quickly rebuilt, christening it Strateburgum (town of the road). This name appears written for the first time in a text by Grégoire de Tours from the sixth century. Flourishing rapidly under the authority of the bishops, the town was described by the ninth century as noisy and bustling, a good indication of the city's activity.

In February 842 Charles the Bald and his brother Louis, grandsons of Charlemagne, met on the Plain of the Butchers to exchange in Latin and a Germanic dialect the Oaths of Strasbourg, thereby allying themselves against their brother Lothaire.

The Saint-Paul Temple / The Alsacien Museum shop-sign
Petite France under the snow

At the time of the Holy Roman Empire, around 1140, Strasbourg obtained its first municipal charter, then in 1205 became officially an Imperial City. This status assured Strasbourg freedom and important privileges. The local middle class soon rejected domination by the town's bishop, then that of the nobles, and established a democratic system of government which lasted until the Revolution.

The prosperity of the city brought with it important cultural movements. In the thirteenth century Gottfried de Strasbourg wrote one of the masterpieces of medieval German literature, Tristan and Isolde. In 1434 Gutenberg established himself in Strasbourg and perfected a "secret" invention which would turn the world upside down: the printing press. With the rapid dissemination of the Bible and the gospel, the spread of Luther's teaching and that of other writers like Sebastian Brant, author of the Nef des Fous, the Reformation quickly caught on in Strasbourg. By 1560 Strasbourg was a stronghold of Protestantism.

In 1681 the annexation of the city for its "protection" and the proclamation of Strasbourg as a "Royal Free Town" brought the cathedral back under Catholic control, and Louis XIV was able to listen to a

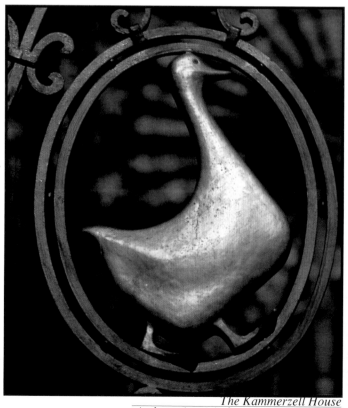

The Kammerzell House
A close view / A shop sign rue Mercière

Te Deum here the twenty-third of October. During his reign and that of Louis XV new construction, notably of the Rohan Palace, changed the city's physical aspect. The Revolution fired the spirits of Strasbourg's inhabitants, and the city provided two of the period's greatest generals: Kellerman and Kléber. It was during this period that a young officer Rouget de Lisle sang for the first time a "*Song of War for the Armies of the Rhine*", soon to become known as "La Marseillaise". De Lisle sang the Marseillaise in the home of de Dietrich, the first mayor chosen under the new constitution.

After a siege of fifty days, with entire neighborhoods set on fire and burned by the more than 200,000 bombs which fell on them, with the Aubette town museum and the Dominican church library completely destroyed, Strasbourg finally surrendered to the Prussian armies on September 27, 1870. The city, along with the rest of Alsace, became German. Reconstruction under the Second Reich was logical and practical, if sometimes not particularly aesthetic. All in all, the city did not suffer as badly as it might have; in fact, the port was even modernized, and the town's cultural life continued to flourish.

During World War I Strasbourg was not directly touched. On November 22, 1918, French troops liberating the city from the several decades long German occupation received a triumphal welcome from the local population.

With the declaration of World War II in September, 1939, many of Strasbourg's residents moved to the southwest of France,

The statue of Gutemberg
The "Cour du Corbeau"

and Hitler's troops entered town June 19, 1940, without firing a shot. The swastika floated over the cathedral which was to remain closed during the entire Occupation. Those residents who returned after 1941 were subjected to an excessive campaign to render Alsace as German as possible, not to mention Allied bombs in August and September of 1944. On November 23, the Second Division lead by General Leclerc liberated Strasbourg.

Pleasure boats leaving from beside the Rohan Palace propose a nautical tour of Strasbourg at its most picturesque. From the boats one views the old houses and many monuments of the city from a different perspective. Of particular charm is the "Petite France" neighborhood of Strasbourg. The name "Petite France" comes from that of a hospital at one time situated here which treated what was called "the French Disease" or syphilis, imported from Italy by the Italian mercenaries of Charles VIII. The French, however, called this illness "the Naples Disease". The boats navigate between half-timbered houses and medieval

The Petite France

structures mirrored in the waters of the Ill river while guides explain the history of Strasbourg in three languages.

There is much too much to say about monuments and buildings worthy of a tourist's interest in Strasbourg. After a visit to the tourist office in the Rue du Dôme just behind the cathedral, the best way to discover the town is simply to stroll through Strasbourg's streets, led by one's imagination in one's search for the city's soul.

Loyal to its traditional role as a crossroads for peoples and ideas, Strasbourg has resolutely turned toward the future, one which from now on will be linked to that of Europe of the twenty-first century.

Consequently, the capital of Alsace has been the headquarters of the Council of Europe since 1949. Its ultramodern building, the Palace of Europe, lies on the banks of the Ill across from the Orangery Park. It is here also that the European Parliament holds its sessions, drafting the laws of the European Community.

The Palace of European Council
The room of the European Parliament

We must not leave Strasbourg without mentioning one of the local glories: Kronenbourg beer. The Kronenbourg brewery can be toured, and on the premises one finds an interesting museum.

The beer, one of the symbols of Alsace, is made from a recipe that has remained unchanged over the years. Sprouted barley is *touraillée* or dried at temperatures which vary depending on the desired color (pale for regular beer, caramel or amber for dark or reddish beer). The malt is then crushed, mixed with water into a paste, and progressively heated in a boiler. The product obtained is then filtered, added to hops, and put in a vat where it will cook for one or two hours to give it the necessary bitterness and aroma. This preparation is, in turn, clarified, cooled, mixed with yeast, and left to ferment for about eight days. At this point the beer, called *green beer*, is transferred to holding tanks. Here the brew ripens, acquiring its sparkling character and its bouquet. After a month the drink will be ready for consumption. The beer is, however, filtered one last time to remove a slight cloudiness and only then appears on your table, ready to be enjoyed.

In June 1664, Jerome Hatt, recently married and honored with a master brewer's diploma, set up a brewery in the Place du Corbeau (Square of the Crow) in Strasbourg. To avoid having his cellars flooded by the Ill, the master brewer soon moved his business to the suburb of Cronenbourg. The rest is history...

Hop's harvest / The master's eye
A hop vat / The holding tanks in the Kronenbourg Museum

THE PAGAN WALL

Let us consider now the twists and turns of time as we look at the distant past. Around the Mount Saint Odile snakes for over six miles a wall of sandstone blocks, originally held together by oak joints and finely fitted at each end. These blocks were cut from nearby rock by wedging pieces of wood into cracks in the stone. Once the wedges became wet the wood expanded splitting the rock. Thanks to studies done in the 1960s and 1970s, it is known that this area was inhabited 2500 years B.C. and that the wall was constructed in two stages, the first during the Middle Bronze Age and the second during the Late Bronze Age. There is much conjecture, however, about the purpose of this construction. Was it a fortress? or a sanctuary? Perhaps, the wall was part of a structure serving both purposes at once. Ancient chroniclers of the Mount Saint Odile spoke of the existence of an elliptical pagan temple located on the site of a still-standing local monastery that is strangely reminiscent of the alignment of monumental rocks at Stonehenge in Great Britain.

The pagan wall

THE MOUNT SAINT-ODILE

Perched on a peak of rose colored sandstone, surrounded by fir trees, the Mount Saint Odile dominates the region. Like Goethe, Barrès, and so many others, one owes a visit to the place dedicated to the patron saint of Alsace.

Aldaric, third holder of the ducal throne of Alsace, was a violent and quick-tempered man. When his wife the Duchesse Bereswinde, long sterile, finally gave birth to a blind daughter, instead of the desired male heir, the Duke decided to do away with the child. To save the girl from her father's wrath, the

The Mount Sainte-Odile

Duchesse confided the child to her nurse who spirited her away to the Palma Convent. The child had to wait a good decade before Saint Ehrard, Bishop of Ratisbonne, came to baptize her. At this moment the child Odile, whose name means "the light of God", recovered her sight. Odile's brother Hugues brought her back to their father's castle Hohenbourg. Aldaric, mad with rage, killed Hugues and tried to marry his daughter who escaped, finding shelter in a rock that miraculously opened up before her. Finally, touched by Divine Grace, Aldaric repented, giving Odile his castle so that she could

establish Alsace's first convent. When Odile died in 720 church bells throughout the land rang in unison for her.

Numerous calamities followed the death of Odile. The convent was beset by no less than seventeen wars and fires. During the French Revolution the convent buildings were denied their sprirtual functions and finally sold. In 1794 revolutionaries wanting to profane the tomb of Saint Odile found that her relics had disappeared, to be returned by the faithful only in 1800. The Bishop of Strasbourg returned to the convent its spiritual mandate in 1853.

Many times restored, the convent buildings include a twelfth century chapel, erected on the site where Odile died. The chapel contains the Saint's tomb, a sarcophagus from the eighth century, re-done in the fourteenth century after Charles IV removed the relics it contained. When the sarcophagus was opened, onlookers saw that Odile's body was still intact.

One of the site's curiosities is a seventeenth century multiple sided sundial from a destroyed abbey that indicates the time for twenty-four locations in the world, from India to the Congo by way of Santiago de Compostela and Mexico.

The monastery, aside the rock / The sundial
The inside yard of the monastery

THE DONON

Between the Lorraine and Alsace, not too far from the Mount Saint Odile, the forest-covered Donon Plateau rises up 1009 meters above sea level. The plateau's name comes from "Dun" or "Dunos" which means "The Mountain". Since the seventeenth century successive archeological digs have uncovered numerous indications that this was once a place of worship. In fact, the Leuques, Médiomatriques, and Triboques, all Celtic tribes whose territories met here, considered the summit of the plateau a magic site.

At the summit, in a sort of amphitheater, rise reproductions of seven monolithic monuments, each one representing a god. The originals are preserved in the museum at Epinal. Nearby there was a sanctuary, constructed in 103 A.D. by the Roman Emperor Trajan, dedicated to Mercury. At the very top crowning the summit sits a small temple built in 1869 with donations from the public. On the stone slabs surrounding the temple one finds a remarkable collection of fantastic graffiti, some of which date from more than 200 years ago.

The "Temple", built in 1869
The celtic monuments

THE "ROUTE DU VIN" starts in the outskirts of Strasbourg. The road will lead us across vineyards and a sloping landscape of medieval villages and picturesque towns, the region of storks and half-timbered houses. The Romans planted the first vine stocks in the second century A.D. Since, these stocks have received constant attention from Alsatian wine producers. Some 120 million bottles of Sylvaner, Gewurztraminer, Pinot, Riesling, Muscat, and Tokay (this latter apparently brought from Hungary originally) are produced each year to grace the tables of consumers, three quarters of whom are French.

Alsatian wines are little known, and we cannot counsel visitors strongly enough to discover the diversity of local vintages while touring the different places they come from, a diversity that makes these products rich and varied. From Pinot Noir or Blanc to Chasselas, Edelzwicker, Tokay (Pinot Gris), or Muscat, they all accompany beautifully the treasures of Alsatian cuisine: foie gras, *Bäckeoffe*, *Schifele*, *Spätzele*, and *Flamekücke*.

120 million of bottles in a Year...

Our first stop on the Route du Vin is Molsheim, forever famous in the hearts of automobile lovers for housing the factory of Ettore Bugatti. Built on a Gallo-Roman village, this fortified town has kept one gate of the ancient ramparts which is called the Blacksmith's Tower and dates from 1412. Also preserved is the Metzig, a large Renaissance building, constructed by the butcher's guild around 1525. The Jesuit church, now a parish church, was erected around 1615 and garnered praise from Louis XIV during his visit in 1683.

About three kilometers further lies Mutzig, one of the "beer towns", whose large Wagner brewery was founded in 1812. The fortified town gate, a vestige of the old walls, dates from the thirteenth century.

Obernai, several minutes farther by car, is equally known for its beer but even more so for its typical Alsatian charm. First a summer residence for the Duke Aldaric, father of Saint Odile, the town would later join the Décapole. During the Thirty Years War Obernai was almost entirely destroyed and did not regain its prosperity until Alsace was annexed by France under the Treaty of Westphalia. The center of town presents the perfect picture of Alsace: half-timbered houses, bay windows, pitched rooftops with dormer windows, etc. The town hall dates from approximately 1520, while the Kapellturm, seventy-two meters high, is all that remains of a medieval chapel. Each year toward mid-October the grape harvest festival brings into the streets a colorful mix of ancient costumes and wagons. A sight not to be missed!

Not far from here the town of Barr also holds its grape harvest festival, one that is particularly appreciated by local wine producers. One should take advantage of a stop in Barr to visit the admirable collection of furniture and earthenware found in the Folie Marco Museum which is housed in a building dating from the eighteenth century.

Following the Route du Vin, we soon arrive at Andlau with its memories of Saint Richarde and her bear. Charles the Fat, her terrifyingly jealous husband, accused Richarde of committing adultery with a bishop and repudiated her. To prove her innocence, Richarde, submitting herself to God's judgement, walked on hot coals. Afterwards she left the court and fled to the Andlau Valley. Soon, in a dream, Richarde received the order to

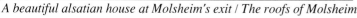

A bay-windowed house in Molsheim

A beautiful alsatian house at Molsheim's exit / The roofs of Molsheim

found a convent at "the spot where a bear would scratch the earth." Having seen a bear burying its dead baby, Richarde went to the site, brought the dead animal back to life and then buil a convent at that very location. According to another story, the abbey was founded in 880 and called Eléon, deformed later into Andlau. One may still visit the church building which, with it: sculpted frieze and magnificent door, represents one of the high points of Alsatian Romanesque art.

One finds a bear in the coat of arms of the town of Dambach located several kilometers away. Surrounded by ramparts and moats, this medieval village boasts half-timbered gabled house: as well as a chapel dedicated to Saint Sebastian, site of ar ancient pilgrimage that still takes place today.

One of the fortified gates , and the ramparts of Dambach / A balcony in Dambach
The church of Blienschwiller, surrounded by the grape-vines of the "Route du Vin"

SÉLESTAT,

several kilometers off the Route du Vin on the road between Strasbourg and Mulhouse, is the ideal spot for a rest stop and a hike to see Haut Koenigsbourg Castle and its surroundings. A charter dating from the eighth century mentions Sélestat as an important Frankish town, and it is here that Charlemagne spent Christmas in 775. Frederick II fortified the town which became an Imperial City in the thirteenth century and a member of the Décapole in the fourteenth. During the fifteenth and sixteenth centuries Sélestat became one of Europe's important intellectual centers in which the philosophy known as humanism was developed. The first southern German university was founded in this town. Furthermore, Beatus Rhenanus, a companion of Erasmus, assembled here a collection of over 2000 philosophical and literary books, preserved today in the Humanist Library which was once the old wheat market hall. Sélestat can be proud to possess this collection, still complete and intact, for it is unique in the world.

The town offers many other attractions conjuring up dreams of times gone by: The Witches Tower, part of the old wall where women accused of witchcraft were imprisoned, or Saint George's Church, built in the thirteenth century on the site of a Carolingian chapel. The church's architecture juxtaposes Romanesque foundations, a Gothic nave, and a Renaissance pulpit.

Other sites include the Saint-Foy Church from the twelfth century, built with subsidies from the Emperor Frederick Barbarossa on the circular crypt of an earlier chapel, the New Tower, and the Clock Tower, one of the four gates of the town's second wall (1280). Finally, there is the Commanderie Saint Jean, founded in the thirteenth century by the Order of Saint Jean, with its fine example of Renaissance architecture.

If you are lucky enough to be in Sélestat the second Sunday of August, do not for any reason miss the "Corso Fleuri", a festival during which floats covered with thousands of dahlias drive through the wonderfully festive streets. This unforgettable spectacle celebrated its fiftieth birthday in 1989.

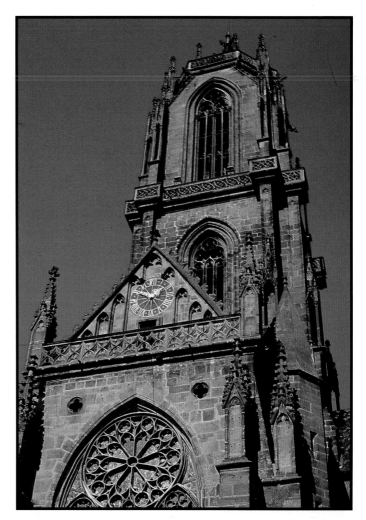

Sélestat: The Saint-George's church
The "Corso fleuri" / The Market Place | *Next pages: The Haut Kœnigsbourg castle*

HAUT-KŒNIGSBOURG

From Sélestat one sees to the west a formidable castle perched on a wooded hill. This is Haut-Kœnigsbourg, reconstructed by order of William II at the beginning of the century by Bodo Ebhard, the German Viollet-le-Duc. After Versailles and the Eiffel Tower the castle is the most frequently visited monument in France.

The castle was originally built in the eleventh century by the Hohenstaufen. During the fourteen hundreds the castle became the hide-out of Henry and Regnard May de Lambsheim whose favorite pastime consisted of looting and ravaging the towns of the nearby Rhine Valley. In 1426 the towns of Basel, Colmar, and Strasbourg gathered a powerful army, besieged the castle, and captured it on October 29. The castle became one of the residences of the Swiss Counts of Thierstein for a time before being taken and burned by the Swedish during the Thirty Years War. This eagle's nest was abandoned and slowly fell into ruin. In 1865 the town of Sélestat acquired Haut-Koenigsbourg and presented it as a gift to William II who had the castle restored. This restoration was at the origin of a great debate that had the famous cartoonist and Alsatian writer Hansi sarcastically asking one of his favorite targets, Professor Knatschke, "Why are the Alsatians complaining? We have replaced the old and miserable ruins with a superb new feudal castle." In fact, Bodo Ebhard did not skimp on the crenellated towers.

"I did not desire it," the Emperor had engraved on one of the castle's chimneys in 1917. He was referring to World War I, not to the overly zealous restoration of the castle.

These complaints aside, Haut Kœnigsbourg is undeniably of historical interest and the joy of visitors and film makers alike; Jean Renoir shot The Grand Illusion with Eric Von Stroheim and Pierre Fresnay here.

Like them, one can stroll along the ramparts and from high up one of the towers contemplate the superb panorama stretching from the Vosges Mountains to the Black Forest. In room after room one may admire antique furniture, originals and copies, magnificent Alsatian earthen cookware, collections of armor and medieval weapons, and above all else imagine with accuracy the life led by men and women of the time.

Haut-Kœnigsbourg castle: an alsatian stove / The lorrainesse bedroom
The festival Hall

Alsace is sprinkled with castles, either in ruins or restored. Many are in northern Alsace, but a good number of those in the south are not far from the Route du Vin and are relatively easy to visit. Near Haut Kœnigsbourg the castle of Ortenbourg, for example, still looks proud thrusting from its rocky peak above the plain. Constructed at the end of the thirteenth century by Rodolphe de Habsbourg, the fortress permitted surveillance of the entire region from the top of its five sided keep. All the same, the swedish managed to burn the castle in 1632. The following year the same Swedes dismantled at Ramstein Castle, a bit lower down the hill, a siege tower built by an imperial bailiff who attacked Ortenbourg back in 1293. The tower was equiped with a giant crossbow, positioned with a huge jack, that fired its bows toward the besieged castle.

The area of Mount Saint Odile is also rich with fortified sites, like the castles of Ottrott (Rathsamhausen and Lutzelbourg) which sit facing one another, separated by a moat. In the mid-twelve hundreds the inhabitants of the two castles were at war. At the end of the sixteenth century, however, the two fortresses were united by the Rathsamhausen and today are being restored.

We must also cite the three castles of Drestein, with their mirky history, as well as those of Klagenfelds and Birkenfelds, built by the Bishop of Strasbourg toward the middle of the eleventh century.

Another, Landsberg, was constructed on an ancient Roman palace. Its destruction by fire provoked by the Swedish during the Thirty Years War left traces still seen today in the stone.

Finally, let us finish this brief tour of Alsace's castles with Spesburg and Haut-Andlau. The former was the residence of the abbey of Andlau's lawyer, and the latter, dating from 1337, once housed Franz d'Ettinghofen, a forest ranger who slew the last bear in the Vosges Mountains in 1695.

Another Alsatian castle meriting our attention is Kintzheim, home of the "Volerie des Aigles".

The Ortenbourg Castle / The Ottrot Castle
The Haut-Kœnigsbourg Castle entry / The Andlau Castle

THE CASTLE OF KINTZHEIM, at an altitude of 280 meters, dominates the surrounding forest. Built for the most part in the thirteen and fourteen hundreds, the castle was also to be destroyed by the Swedes during the Thirty Years War. The ruins, now strengthened, shelter some sixty birds of prey that master falconers have taught to delight visitors every afternoon in front of the castle's keep. It is not often one sees vultures, eagles, and kites swoop to within several meters of one's head. Among the attractions is a small African vulture with a very special technique for feeding himself. He bombards the plaster shell enclosing his food with stones until it breaks, permitting him finally to devour his dinner.

Castle of Kintzheim: the "Volerie des Aigles"
A Royal Eagle / Lou's hunt: a family business !

From the "Volerie des Aigles" the road to visit "La Montagne des Singes" is indicated. Here, nearly 300 Barbary apes live in the semi-liberty of twenty-four hectares of forest. Introducing these animals to the region might seem a delicate matter, but it must be remembered that they come from the high plateaus of Morocco and Algeria where climatic conditions are similar to those of this part of Alsace. The Kintzheim region enjoys a very dry micro-climate; only about 600 millimeters of rain fall here every year. The apes live peacefully in groups of twelve to 200 individuals and reproduce once a year in the spring. These animals are very sociable and readily frequent the 800 meters of paths that crisscross the park, waiting for popcorn offerings from the tourists. One may also surprise the apes bathing, playing, or diving into their small pond. Mademoiselle Merz, followed by her labrador Caracho, watches over this micro-society, all the while studying it in the company of researchers come from around the world.

Thanks to this park, Alsace has become an exporter of the apes, not the least of Alsatian paradoxes. Perhaps one day the Kintzheim colony of apes will make contact with the forty members of the same species that have lived for over a thousand years on the Rock of Gibraltar.

Suspicion on pop-corn
Bath time

From Kintzheim we rejoin the Route du Vin where several charming medieval towns await us. On arriving at Bergheim visitors pass under the Ribeauvillé Tower, a gateway to the old city fortified in the fourteenth century. This small wine producing village with its houses enclosed by a number of old towers possesses a Linden tree, planted along a roadway in the Middle Ages, that seems eternal. The choir and apse of the red sandstone church are in the Gothic style, but the rest of the building dates from the eighteenth century.

Before arriving at Ribeauvillé we will stop at Hunawihr, a town guarded over by its fortified church. The town's name is said to derive from "Huno" and "Hune", an upper class couple from the seventh century. The wife was a relative of Saint Odile whom we have already met. Site of a pilgrimage to Saint Hune, the town became in the Middle Ages the property of a noble family by the same name. Construction of the town's fortified church is attributed to this family. The church, dominated by a massive tower which is both belfry and keep, is protected by a hexagonal wall dating from the fourteenth century that contains only one entry but six bastions. In 1672 freedom of religion was accepted here and even today mixed Catholic-Protestant couples come from all over Alsace to have their marriages consecrated.

Should you arrive in Ribeauvillé the Sunday preceding the eighth day of September, you will find yourself having more and more difficulty distinguishing reality from dreams. This is the annual wandering minstrel's festival, called Pfifferdaj or Pfiffertag. Why a brotherhood of minstrels in Ribeauvillé? Why the historic parade? Why is there a fountain of wine? All exist today because of a fife player. Long ago this traveling musician honored the nobles of the region by organizing a fantastic parade with jugglers, trained dogs, bears in tutus, tightrope walking monkeys, and drum playing cats. Sad about having lost his fife during the festivities, the musician was rewarded by the nobles with a sack full of gold, and ever since the minstrels have made merry

A street in Bergheim

Acording to the tradition, blue houses are dedicated to Virgin Mary

Ribeauvillé: stork's nest with the Grand-Ribeaupierre castle in the background
The church of Hunawihr

in Ribeauvillé.

Nestled at the foot of the Vosges Mountains and watched over by the old castles that tower above the town, Ribeauvillé is famous as much for its Riesling as for Carola, its natural spring water. The town was the fief of the very powerful family of the knights of Ribeaupierre or Rappolstein. After becoming attached to the royal domain during the reign of Frederick II Barbarossa, Ribeauvillé was granted town status, a position which brought many advantages up to the time France annexed the town under Louis XIV. A stroll through the main street (Grande Rue) brings one to the Butcher's Tower, a belfry remaining from the town's ancient internal fortifications built in the thirteenth century. Stops at the town's many fountains, two in the Renaissance style, are a perfect way to refresh oneself. On the hills surrounding Ribeavillé the Ribeaupierre had three fortresses built which were abandoned after the construction in town of a more comfortable abode. 500 meters above sea level le Grand Ribeaupierre or Saint Ulrich Castle stands with its keep from the thirteenth century on a rocky peak facing the mountain. This edifice is a remarkable specimen of the fortified palaces of the Middle Ages. Perched on a neighboring hill crest is the Petit-Ribeaupierre or Girsberg Castle, impressive despite its relatively small size. Finally, Haut Ribeaupierre or Altenkastel rises 645 meters above the village, and from its crenelated tower one discovers a splendid panorama.

Three different views of Ribeauvillé

RIQUEWIHR

Following the sinuous roads of the Route du Vin between the green leaves of Alsace's most famous vineyards, we arrive soon in Riquewihr. This jewel has survived intact the many wars and struggles that have dotted its history. Merovingian sarcophagi help us imagine the age of this small town. Already in the year 1000 the town's prosperity was a source of pride to its inhabitants as is illustrated by its old name, Richovilare (rich village). From the Counts of Eguisheim, first lords of the village, the town passed to the Horbourgs who built its first wall during the thirteenth century. In the fifteen hundreds Riquewihr was ceded to the Counts of Wurtemberg-Montbéliard who raised a second wall and built a castle in 1539. During this period the town experienced an astonishing prosperity thanks to its wine which in 1643 was declared the "most noble of the land". Riquewihr is still one of Alsace's main wine producing communities, and the growers exploit the eight different soils of Schoenenberg, Sporen and other hills.

Riquewihr: the Dolder gate
Next pages: Riquewihr, circled by the grape-vine

In Main street (Grand' Rue) / The Press-Zimmer sign, designed by Hansi
The Courtyard of the storks

Once in town, only several meters away from the town hall, one finds the castle, earlier in ruins but now restored in order to house the Postal Museum, home of an impressive retrospective on post offices from Gallo-Roman times to the present. Ascending the main street toward the Dolder Gate is a veritable voyage through the sixteenth and seventeenth centuries. Most of the houses along the way have their date of construction engraved above the door which makes dating these structures simple. At the beginning of the street the Liebrich house, with its Courtyard of the Storks, offers visitors wooden balconies overflowing with flowers, a well dating from 1603 and an enormous wine press from 1817. Across the street the Berel House possesses a handsome bay window from 1514. A bit farther up the street, the Preiss-Zimmer sign designed by Hansi announces the ancient Auberge de l'Etoile. Behind this old inn lies an alley leading to the Court of the Wine Growers where the all powerful wine producers guild had its headquarters. An inscription in German asks God for protection from fires.

Through a small street across from the Preiss-Zimmer house one enters the Tithing Court, once belonging to the Ribeaupierre nobles. It was here that the lords collected the tithe, a tax paid by handing over a percentage of the harvest. Close to the Dolder Gate is the Court of the Jews, the old Jewish neighborhood at the beginning of the sixteenth century. Nearby, the Tower of the Thieves, massive and fearsome, served as prison and torture chamber. Inside one finds the instruments used to make the condemned beg for mercy as well as a dungeon and solitary confinement chamber.

In the thirteenth century the Dolder Gate housed watchmen and body guards but now serves as the Archeological Society Museum with a collection of weapons, furniture, and ancient objects.

A 1560 fountain facing the Dolder Gate
The Main street (Grand'Rue)

KAYSERSBERG

From the Roman period when it was called Caesaris Mons to the present, Kaysersberg's name has always meant "The Mount of the Emperors". Henry VII, son of the Emperor Frederick II, bought the village and its castle in order to fortify the area, thereby firmly blocking the Weiss Valley through which one gains access to the Bonhomme Pass. A free town by the end of the thirteenth century, Kaysersberg joined the Décapole. If the Tokay grape is the specialty of the area, it is because Lazarus Schwendi, an imperial bailiff returning from a military campaign in Hungary, brought back from the Tokay region several vines which he gave to the town. Other well-known men have been born or lived in Kaysersberg, among them the famous preacher Johann Geiler, the Reformer Matthäus Zell, and, of course, Albert Schweitzer. In memory of the latter the town has a sister city in Lambaréné, Gabon where the doctor built his hospital. The fortified bridge over the Weiss river is a unique example of military architecture in Alsace. From its crenelated guardrail pierced with slots for firing weapons, one's eyes wander over the typical medieval houses. Lastly, we cannot leave without a visit to Sainte Croix Church with its grand altar surmounted by a choir screen of sculpted wood made in 1518 by the Colmar craftsman Jean Bongartz. The Crucifixion is surrounded by twelve panels illustrating the Last Supper and the important themes of the New Testament.

The house of Albert Schweitzer / The choir screen in Sainte-Croix church
Old timbered houses of Kaysersberg

COLMAR

Charlemagne and later his son Louis the Debonair were frequent visitors to the Villa Columbarium, a vast Carolingian complex built in the Rhine plain on the banks of the Lauch. At the center of the villa a tower served as a dovecoat and perhaps gave its name to the town. The domain of the "Colombes" or doves became Columbara and then Colmar. As part of the Holy Roman Empire the town received numerous visits from Frederick I Barbarossa as well as from Frederick II who decreed the town an Imperial City and built its first wall at the beginning of the thirteenth century. The inhabitants of Colmar were very astonished to see Frederick II arrive one day with camels, eunuchs, and veiled women, forgetting that he was also King of Sicily.

At this time Colmar was openly defying the Bishop of Strasbourg who would have liked to have annexed the prosperous town. Jean Roesselmann, son of a tanner, was provost much to the vexation of the local nobles who formed a pact with the Bishop and ran him out. Roesselmann took refuge with Rodolphe de Habsbourg, the future emperor. With the latter's support Roesselmann was able to retake the town. The following year, however, the provost was killed in a skirmish with the Bishop who was again attempting to take the city. The town bourgeoisie, however, managed to keep the authority within the municipality

The "Maison au Fer Rouge", in the rue des Marchands

and, therefore, assured the town's prosperity.

On August 28, 1354, Colmar and nine other Alsatian towns founded the Décapole which assured its members assistance in case of agression or internal disturbances and sought to resolve peacefully disputes between adhering towns. Political and economic stability reigned for many years, proof of which lies in the many Renaissance structures built during this period. During the Thirty Years War, however, the emperor demanded that inhabitants participating in the Reformation leave the city. The ensuing exodus created serious problems for Colmar since many rich and influential Protestant families were forced to leave. In 1635 Colmar enjoyed French protection while remaining within the German empire. Louis XIV had his troops occupy the town in 1673, and after the victory of Turenne over the Imperial forces in 1675, Colmar swore loyalty to the king of France in 1679.

Colmar suffered little during the Revolution but gave Napoleon one of his greatest generals, Jean Rapp.

After 1870 and during the entire German annexation Colmar's loyalty to France could not be doubted. Hansi, a writer and ferocious cartoonist born in the

region in 1873, became the bard of French patriotism and of a French Alsace. One may still admire some of his superb signs in the neighborhood near the Dominican church.

Little Venise is one of Colmar's most picturesque spots. The ancient houses are reflected by the waters of the Lauch, among flowers and trees, while contented ducks and swans wait for tourists. Little Venise is surrounded by the Fishery quarter, so called because of the large hoop nets the fishermen left in the river before going to sell their catch, and the Krutenau neighborhood of the produce sellers. Here one finds two works by Bartholdi, another local celebrity. One is a monument to Jean Roesselmann and the other the Fountain of the Wine Grower, dedicated to the glories of Alsatian vineyards.

Another Bartholdi monument, one in memory of Lazarus Schwendi, stands in the middle of the Ancient Customs Square. According to legend, Schwendi is supposed to have brought the Tokay grape back from Hungary. His figure proudly clutches a bunch of these grapes. Across from Schwendi the Koifhus, with its colorful roof tiles from the seventeenth century, housed the customs office. The office is comprised of

Little Venise

two buildings, the first of which was built in 1480 and served as a warehouse for taxed goods as well as a meeting hall for the aldermen and representatives of the Décapole. The second building, constructed at the end of the sixteenth century, boasts an exterior staircase with slanted sides and an elegant balcony that overlooks the square. In the doorman's small quarters was born the future General Rapp in 1771.

Several steps away down La Rue des Marchands (Merchant Street) one arrives at the Pfister House, built in 1537 by a hatter from Besançon. The bay window and the facade are covered with frescos representing emperors and biblical characters. The building's octagonal staircase tower almost touches a very beautiful house constructed in 1609 and embellished by a wooden balcony and a sculpted figure representing a cloth maker. Behind these two houses one finds the Adolphe House which dates from 1350 and is the oldest in Colmar.

In the Place de la Cathédrale is the old regiment house, constructed in 1575. From the Renaissance loggia the town magistrates took oath, and infamous condemnations were pronounced. Facing this building is the old collegiate church of Saint Martin, called "The Cathedral" by residents of Colmar. Built in the thirteenth and fourteenth centuries on the site of a church begun in the year 1000, this "cathedral" possesses a Gothic nave and two towers, only one of which has been completed. On one wall of the largest tower a sundial carries the inscription Memento Mori ("Remember Death"). The Saint Nicolas portal evokes the story of the legendary fourth century bishop of the same name. The similarity between the three virgins who accompany him and the mad virgins of Strasbourg Cathedral is clear.

The Pfister House / The cloth maker of the next house
Flowered front of a house, rue des Marchands

The Dominican church not far away serves as a temporary home to Martin Schongauer's masterpiece "La Vierge au Buisson de Roses". Painted in 1473, the work should long ago have been returned to its rightful place in the collegiate church of Saint Martin. In this case, however, the temporary lingers on.... The Dominican convent (fifteenth century) houses a library where one finds manuscripts from the Carolingian period in addition to a collection of writings by the Ribeaupierre nobles.

Colmar possesses one of France's most beautiful museums in its Unterlinden Convent. Constructed during the second half of the thirteenth century this Dominican convent was famous for more than five centuries for the mysticism and austerity ruling here. The Revolution dispersed the nuns, and the convent became barracks for a division of mounted soldiers armed with lances. In 1847 the Schongauer Society assumed control of the convent and turned it into a cultural center with a drawing school and a museum now dedicated to medieval art, archeology, folklore and crafts, and the cartoonist Hansi. Among the treasures on exhibit in the museum, the most famous is undoubtedly the Issenheim choir screen painted around 1510 by Matthias Grünewalt (whose real name was probably Mathis Neithardt or Gotthardt).

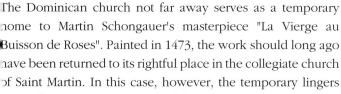

The exterior staircase of the Koifhus / Lazarus Schwendi, by Bartholdi
The Koifhus and its wooden balcony

Several meters from the Unterlinden Museum the Maison des Têtes or House of the Heads, constructed in 1608 by a rich merchant, has now become a restaurant. The house, so named because of the numerous sculpted heads ornamenting its bay window and facade, is one of the musts of any visit to Colmar's old town.

Close views of the House of the Heads / The House of the heads (front)
The Issenheim choir-screen (Unterlinden Museum) *The "Virgin in the rose bush" (Dominican church)*

Four shop-signs, by Hansi

EGUISHEIM

In Eguisheim to the south of Colmar, the medieval streets spiral around the castle. Built on the site of an eighth century fortress constructed by a nephew of Saint Odile, Eguisheim Castle witnessed in 1002 the birth of Bruno, son of Hughes IV and the Countess of Dabo. Bruno of Eguisheim became first Bishop of Toul and then Pope under the name Leo IX. As pope, Leo IX was a great reformer, and it was at the end of his mandate that the orthodox schism occured in 1054.

The village has remained almost completely intact since the sixteenth century with its circular streets following the lines traced by ancient walls. Here one discovers magnificent bay windows on the wood-sided houses, two pretty Renaissance fountains, and ancient tithing courts where the religious men of Pairis, Ebermunster, and Marbach, as well as the Bishop of Strasbourg, would come to claim their share of the harvests. Over Eguisheim loom the three famous towers of Schlossberg: Weckmund, Walhenbourg, and Dabsbourg (eleventh and twelfth centuries). The three castles to which these towers belonged were destroyed in 1466 during the Six Farthings War.

A flowered bay-window / Pope Leo IX
The alsatian plain

TURCKHEIM

"Listen to what I have come to tell you - the church bell has rung ten o'clock - let God give to all a good night...." With these words from another era on Christmas and New Year's Eve and every night from Easter to the fall, Turckheim's night watchman wishes a good evening to residents of this small wine producing town.

On the banks of the Fecht river Turckheim beckons to visitors through the 14th century Porte de France, one of the town's three fortified gates. During the Middle Ages the witches, their pyres waiting, passed through the vault of the Munster Gate on their way to the site of execution a short distance from town. An Imperial Town and member of the Décapole from 1354 on, Turckheim was the key to passage between Colmar and the Munster Valley. The town was notably the site of an important military campaign. On January 5, 1675, Henri de la Tour d'Auvergne, Viscount of Turenne and Marshall of France, crushed Imperial armies here forcing them to retreat to the other side of the Rhine.

Houses of Turckheim
The night watchman

MUNSTER

Following the Fecht River Valley, one of the country's most charming, we arrive soon at Munster, the town that gave its name to one of France's most well-known cheeses. The name comes from that of an abbey founded here in the seventh century by Irish monks that was destroyed during the Revolution (Munster = monastery). In the thirteenth century the residents of Munster, along with those of Soultzeren, Hohrod, Luttenbach, Metzeral, Muhlbach, and other neighboring villages banded together into a metropolitan grouping: the Civitas Monasteriensis (City of Munster). This association joined the Décapole and formed a small independent republic. At the end of the seventeenth century the valley residents took up textiles and the manufacturing of thread with much success. After World War II, however, this industry died out. Munster has now become a health resort.

On the Place du Marché ruins of the ancient abbey buildings still exist, and one can see from here a couple of storks who have chosen the roof of the town hall as home. The birds put on a show that one never tires of watching, particularly when well-installed across the street on the terrace of the restaurant appropriately named "The Stork".

From Munster mountain lovers may hike through the Schlucht pass on the Route des Crêtes, a mountain top road which provides superb panoramas as it leads us toward the Alsatian lake country.

The roof of the town-hall and the ruins of old abbey
Making Munster's cheese

The Amic Pas
View on the Vosges, from the Route des Crête

"LA ROUTE DES CRETES" AND THE LAKES

Traditionally one begins a journey on the Route des Crêtes at Cernay to the west of Mulhouse, then crosses through the Amic Pass, weaving through a forest of fir trees, before arriving at the Grand Ballon, Markstein, and the Hohneck plateau. From here, one crosses through the Schlucht Pass to end up finally at the Bonhomme Pass. For once, however, let us take the road in the other direction in order to complete our journey near Mulhouse.

The creation of this strategic road was decided during World War I by the French High Command which hoped to assure a communications route between the different valleys on the north-south Vosges front. At the Bonhomme Pass we find ourselves 949 meter high at a crossroads between the Lorraine and Alsace. On one of the neighboring summits stands the ruins of Gutembourg Castle, a fortress built at the beginning of the thirteenth century. From there a splendid view and the pure air of the Vosges Mountains awaits us.

Eight kilometers farther, climbing to 1054 meters, we arrive at White Lake whose silvery reflections mirror the steep cliff faces of the surrounding rocks. Several minutes along a path bring us to. Black Lake, formed by a dam constructed on the rubble of an ancient glacier.

Following the Route des Crêtes up to an altitude of 1139 meters we come to the "Lo Schluy" or Schlucht Pass.

Until the nineteenth century only one path connected the pass to the Munster Valley. At this time M. Hartmann, a rich industrialist, had the idea of enlarging the path in order to transport more easily his merchandise toward the Lorraine. Napoleon III supported the plan, but nearly twenty-seven years passed before the project was completed. By the beginning of the twentieth century even a little electric cog train was being built. Inaugurated in the spring of 1907, the little train was short-lived because of World War I hostilities.

Graced with a legend of its own, the Hohneck Peak is one of the highest in the

The White Lake

Vosges, rising to 1361 meters. On one side of the mountain, amid springs and meadows, is the Frankentalkeller, also called "Dagobert's Grotto". In this rocky crevice, legend tells us, the good King Dagobert, who wore his breeches backwards, hid from his enemies one day. Supporting this claim is a now almost indetectable path connecting the Hohneck with Stolz Ablas called the Königspfad or King's Way. Between Markstein, where one can peacefully ski in winter, and the rounded mountain top called the Ballon de Guebwiller lies the Lac du Ballon with its marvelous stories, including one about a giant trout. According to the story, on the mossy

GUEBWILLER

From the Grand Ballon, or Ballon de Guebwiller, which rises above Alsace to an altitude of 1424 meters, one discovers the grandiose scenery of the Vosges Mountains and the Black Forest.

In the valley below the eighth century saw monks from the Abbey of Murbach arrive to clear the land. In 1182 construction began on a basilica around which a small community would grow up. By 1270 commerce was thriving, and Guebwiller built its town walls. At the end of the thirteenth century and during all of the fourteenth, Guebwiller was one of the most important Alsatian towns. Thanks to a woman named Brigitte Schick the town was able to fend off an attack

back of the trout grows a fir tree which should tell us something about the age of the monstrous fish! Another story informs us that Attila's treasure is buried in the deep slime at the bottom of the lake. The true history of the lake is not uninteresting. In 1699 Vauban had a canal dug in order to facilitate the transportation of materials necessary for the construction of Neuf-Brisach fort. In 1702 a dike was also erected and then forgotten about once construction on the fort was terminated. The 21st of December, 1740, brought torrential rains which burst the dike. The town of Guebwiller below owes its salvation only to its ancient fortifications which channeled the mad torrents of water away from the village.

Various sights of the Ballon d'Alsace

in 1445 by the Ecorcheurs or "skinners", as was called a band of mercenaries from Armagnac ravaging the countryside at the time. On Valentine's Day our heroine, who was having trouble sleeping, heard the brutes preparing to attack the town ramparts. Quickly she lit some bundles of straw on fire in order to alert the town's inhabitants who were then able to repell the invaders. The ladders and cords of the attackers are still religiously kept at the Saint Léger Church, one of the most beautiful examples of Romanesque architecture in Alsace. Guebwiller's other church, Notre Dame, a jewel constructed in 1785 by Gabriel Ignace Ritter, is in the Austrian Baroque style. Splendid homes line the streets of Guebwiller, but the facade of the town hall is particularly worth noticing. One sees a very beautiful bay window comprised of five sides and a niche sheltering the Virgin Mary who still watches over the abode of Hesser, a draper and first occupant of the building in 1514.

Fontaine of Saint-Léger (1735) / Saint-Léger church
Around Guebwiller

Rising from the fields eight kilometers from Guebwiller is Thierenbach Chapel, site of a very important and ancient pilgrimage. Inside the chapel a statue of Our Lady of the Seven Sorrows is continously lit by numerous candles, and one may admire an astonishing collection of naive ex-votos, the oldest of which dates from 1680.

During the Middle Ages another nearby pilgrimage attracted crowds of the faithful to Thann, a destination almost as popular as Santiago de Compostela. History tells us that Thiébaut, a saintly man and Bishop of Gubbio in Umbria, left his episcopal ring to his most faithful servant who was originally from the Lorraine. While trying to remove the ring before the burial, the man tore off one of his master's fingers. Fitting the ring into his pilgrim's stick, he arrived in 1161 at the Thur Valley where he fell asleep at the foot of a fir tree. Upon waking the man found that the stick had become firmly attached to the tree which had three stars shining from its top. Count Engelhard de Ferrette saw the occurrence from Engelsburg, his castle, and ran to experience the miracle: God had decided to give the land a relic of Saint Thiébaut.

Construction on the collegiate church, or cathedral as it is called by the residents of Thann, started at the beginning of the fourteenth century but was not completed until the end of the fifteenth. The church illustrates the development of the Gothic style from its beginning to the period called flamboyant. The main portal, a veritable book in stone, recounts with more than 500 sculpted characters the life of the Virgin Mary. A statue of Saint Thiébaut blessing the town crowns the portal. The lacy stonework of the tower and spire rise 76 meters into the sky. Inside, the nave occupies an almost perfect square (23 meters long by 22 meters high), and the stained glass windows recount the story of man searching for God. In the chapel of the Virgin the baby Jesus holds in his hand, hidden behind his mother's back, a cluster of grapes. Sculpted in the fifteenth century, this is the Virgin of Wine Growers. After leaving the church, glance at the town hall. This building is the work of a certain Jean-Baptiste Kléber, an architect at the time, who was to become one of the Empire's most famous generals.

The history of Thann is so rich that it would take a book to tell it all. Let us end simply by stating that there still exists a Count of Thann; the title belongs, in fact, to the Grimaldis of Monaco!

Our Lady of the Seven Sorrows
Thierenbach Chapel

Thann Collegiate-church: The choir stained-glass windows / The spire
The main portal / Saint-Thiebault fountain

MULHOUSE

The Tower of Europe, from which one sees the entire city, symbolizes the Mulhouse of today. With its sights set on the future, the metropolis of southern Alsace is as much an economic as cultural crossroads between France, Germany, and Switzerland. But if the city offers a modern and dynamic vision, Mulhouse is nonetheless proud of what remains of its past, much of which was erased during World War II. The city possesses in its extraordinary museums cultural and technological riches most towns would boast about having.

The site has been populated ever since prehistory although it never interested the Romans, unlike the rest of Alsace. Frederick Barbarossa, on the other hand, encouraged the development of the town in the twelfth century. Mülhausen (town of the windmill) declared itself independent from the yoke of the Bishop of Strasbourg and obtained in 1308 the status of Imperial City. The Devil's Tower, in which women accused of witchcraft were imprisoned, and the Nessel Tower, reconstructed at the beginning of the century, are the only vestiges of the Episcopal Palace. The city joined the Décapole and began to develop commercial rather than agricultural activities due to the lack of fertile soil.

In the fifteenth century peace was disrupted by a series of wars, including the "Six Farthings War". A miller who had been denied by a merchant of the Mulhouse bourgeoisie his salary of six farthings had his case dismissed from court. At that point Pierre de Reguisheim, the captain of the guard for the three Eguisheim castles, took up the miller's cause. There followed a war that finally came out in Mulhouse's favor but which lasted several years, during which two of the Eguisheim castles were destroyed.

Until 1445 the town was governed by a council of nobles and patricians. After this date the influence of the town's guilds dominated city politics, and trade developed rapidly with Basel and other Swiss cantons.

Luther appealed to the residents of Mulhouse who had already been attracted by the sermons of Nicolas Prugner, a prior from the city's Augustine monastery, who preached the ideas of the Reformation. The town's inhabitants converted en masse, and mass was abolished in 1529.

The Tower of Europe | *Saint-Etienne Temple's spire / One of the glass-tinted windows: Jonas and the whale (XVI century)*

grouping of Swiss provinces.

The tiny republic experienced a period of independence and economic development, thanks in great part to the opening in 1746 of a factory for printing cloth. The business rapidly developed as did imitators of the printed calico called "indiennes". The cloth was for a time quite fashionable and even exported. The French Revolution did not affect the town too much although the inhabitants were generally sympathetic to its ideals. Hence, the statue in the square before the town hall was topped with one of the symbols of the Revolution, a Phrygian bonnet. On this square, since rebaptized Reunion Square, took place in 1798 the Festival of Reunion celebrating Mulhouse's decision to join the Republic and the subsequent lifting of a customs blockade which was paralyzing business.

After the turmoil of this period business boomed for Mulhouse, spurred on by innovations of the Industrial Revolution. In 1826 the Industrial Society of Mulhouse, founded by twenty-two industrialists, opened institutes of design, chemistry, weaving and cloth making, and inaugurated the first commerce school in France. Demographically speaking, Mulhouse boomed also, growing from 9530 inhabitants in 1815 to 65000 in 1870.

The textile industry did not lose its predominance in the local economy until after World War I when weapons manufacturing plants and electricity concerns were set up. Potassium mining was also developed at this time.

During World War II the Nazis harassed the merchant class, expulsed industrialists and priests, closed the synagogue and confessional schools and rebaptized the Rue du Sauvage (Savage Street) Rue Adolf Hitler, amusing the city's residents

Mulhouse severed its ties with the Décapole and when Alsace was attached to France was considered as belonging to the

The Bollwerk tower (XIV century)
The Guillaume Tell restaurant shop-sign

who, otherwise, had to deal daily with forced conscription into the German army and deportations. Air-raids brought ruin and desolation to the city, particularly one on May 11, 1944, that destroyed many more civilian targets than military.

Mulhouse was liberated in November, 1944, but pounded from then on regularly by German artillery. After the war the city had to be for the most part rebuilt, and unfortunately, there was not always enough consideration given to originality and aesthetics. One finds, however, magnificent gardens, hidden between the walls of the city, and public parks pleasant for strolling. The Salvator park contains an auditorium where one may listen to concerts while the "Jardin des Senteurs" permits the sight impaired to appreciate flowers, grouped together by odour, as well as to learn about them thanks to Braille inscriptions on the panels near each specimen. But the most beautiful park of Mulhouse is the zoological and botanical garden created in 1868 and occupying twenty-five hectares. This park is seen each year by some 400,000 visitors. Among the thousand animals or so that live in this verdant zoo are bisons, bears, reindeer, wapitis, monkeys, birds, saurians, and reptiles.

Mulhouse is the Alsatian museum town par excellence. Mulhouse collects its past, its history, its discoveries, its technological innovations, and its glories. The city possesses collections unique in the world that must be seen.

In the Place de la Reunion, miraculously spared during the war, is the Historical Museum. The museum is housed in the old town hall from the sixteenth century with its facade painted by Jean Gabriel in 1699. On the right side of the building hangs a copy of the Klapperstein, a mask made of stone weighing

twelve kilograms. The mask was hung around the neck of scandalmongers and slanderers who were then paraded through

A private garden
Zoological and botanical garden

Four views of the town hall

town seated backwards on an ass. The original mask rests inside the historical museum along with archeological collections and souvenirs of Mulhouse's past including antique furniture, objects of daily use, toys, baubles, signs, coins, and works in gold and silver.

In the Printed Fabric Museum, one discovers the history and technique of this fine art. Everything is explained from the engraving on wooden planks to the copper rollers, as well as the different machines used in the process. The museum archives contain tens of thousands of samples and patterns from the eighteenth century up to the present, not to mention many painted cloths from around the world. There is also an amazing collection of some 800 handkerchiefs, the purpose of which sometimes leaves one wondering: handkerchiefs with military instructions, for teaching the deaf and dumb, English ones with diverse scenes, and, of course, those for people with colds! Mulhouse's museums offer other surprises. The fine arts museum, housed in a handsome eighteenth century building, possesses among other works paintings by Bruegel de Velours, Teniers, Courbet, and Boudin. A whole room is consecrated to the Charles Oulmont donation with its works by Yves Brayer, Van Dongen and Eugène Carrière.

For lovers of exotic fish let us not forget the calm and restful tropical aquarium in Kingersheim.

Historical Museum: home in the Sundgau
Printed Fabrics Museum: alsactian cashmere foulard (1820)
One of the Tropical Aquarium inhabitants

Locomotive 232 U 1 - 1949
French Railway Museum: general view

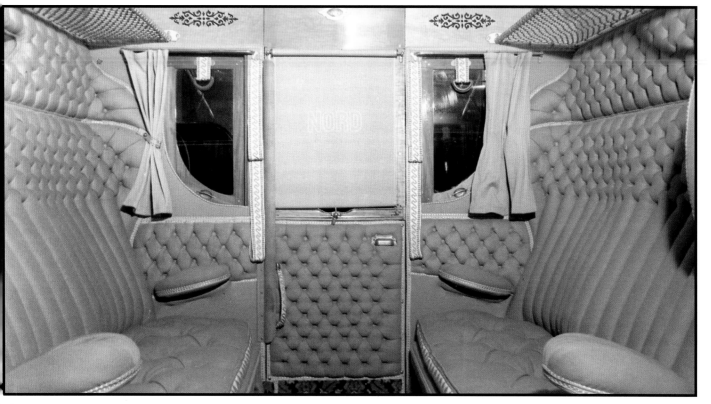

THE FRENCH RAILWAY MUSEUM

Situated in the suburbs of Mulhouse, the Railway Museum evokes the history of the train while creating an altogether indefinable poetry and melancholy. The stars of this reconstructed train station are without a doubt the steam engines, outdated like the Saint-Pierre (1844) with its teak wood or the Sézanne (1847) that could reach sixty kilometers per hour, or monstrous like the 232 U 1 (1949) with its memories of a time when noise, smoke, and the stench of hot oil were part of the trip. Among the equally interesting wagons are the luxurious presidential car with its Lalique crystal and furniture made of precious woods that was used between 1925 and 1971, the imperial wagon of Napoleon III's aides-de-camp, decorated by Viollet-le-Duc, and the historical PR2 car used by General de Gaulle.

Those who are model train buffs are not forgotten either. The collection includes the green BB, setter of a world speed record in 1955, the "salt box" which manoeuvred in stations, and the enormous CC, with its small central cabin, used to pull merchandise trains. They are all here, shamelessly tempting one to become a child again.

1st class coach (1850)
Imperial Train club coach (1856)

THE FIRE-BRIGADE MUSEUM

Next door to the train museum is the Fire-Brigade Museum. Here one finds a unique collection of wooden fire engines from the eighteenth century, of gleaming red vehicles, and of diverse instruments used by the predecessors of today's firemen to fight blazes. Included in the collection are buckets and hoses made of leather, axes, helmets from the world over, gas masks, uniforms from various periods, as well as posters and engravings relating the exploits of firemen. A very early telephone switchboard used for reporting the fires has even been reconstructed. One easily imagines the courage these early firemen had to have as they fought catastrophe, often with insufficient means.

For this wonderful collection we may thank Colonel Ludmann, who spent a large part of his life building it up.

Fire-Brigade Museum: general view
Fire-engine (XIX century) / First-aid truck (beginning XX century)

THE NATIONAL AUTOMOBILE MUSEUM

By general consensus this museum contains the most beautiful collection of automobiles in the world. This museum alone makes a visit to Mulhouse worthwhile. There is no need to be an expert in crankshafts and connecting rods to appreciate the undeniable charm of these eternally elegant roadsters or the devilish attraction of the monstrous race cars. No less than 112 Bugattis sit side-by-side with Rolls Royces, Hispano Suizas, Isotta Fraschinis, Mercedes and other prestigious models. Here one also finds automobiles of famous men like President Poincaré's Panhard X26 or the Delaunay-Belleville of the Russian Czars.

This museum is the only place in the world where one may see permanently exhibited two out of the only six Bugatti Royales ever constructed. One of these two was the personal car of Ettore Bugatti, called the coupé du patron or the boss's car. Over 20,000 square meters 464 cars and 98 different models await visitors, everything from the 1878 steam driven Jacquot to a 1970 Ferrari 312 B. For the most part the cars are all rare items, and one does not dare think of the price or difficulty of putting together this collection today. The Schlumpf brothers undertook this task because of their love for the automobile and in order to dedicate the museum to their mother, a mission that was to take its toll on their factory.

Panhard Dynavia 1948
General view

Bugatti type 41 " Royale " - The "Boss' car "
The last Gordini to have raced in a Grand Prix (M. Trintignant - 1955)
Bugatti type 41 " Royale " limousine

Mercedes-Benz type 330 SLR driven by J.M. Fangio (Le Mans - 1955)
Bugatti type 46 roadster (1936)
Bugatti Atalante type SC (1937)

UPPER ALSACE FOLK MUSEUM

On the road to Guebwiller, between Pulversheim and Bollwiller, exists a curious artificial village where a house from 1480, one from Colmar, and a vineyard keeper's abode sit side by side fifty other Alsacian homes, all of which are different. This is the Upper Alsace Folk Museum, a museum-village where the homes and traditions of the Upper Rhine region are preserved.

Here the marshal takes care of horses, the wheelwright repairs wheels, the clog-maker works his wood, and oils are produced by an oil-maker on the spot. In the homes traditional furniture and earthen cooking pots have replaced modern amenities, and one may sample regional dishes, to be washed down, of course, with local wines.

Two aspects of the Upper Alsace Folk Museum

A house in the Sundgau
Alsace is also foie gras

Typical houses of the Sundgau

THE SUNDGAU

Leaving Mulhouse to the south, toward Altkirch, one follows an ancient Roman road, once a major route of communication in this part of Europe. A ford over the Ill river at Illfurth (meaning ford over the Ill) allows one to cross to the other bank.

Now we are in the Sundgau, a region different from the others in Alsace. Between the Alps and the Rhine, the Sundgau, with its well-kept homes that give the region its own special charm, reminds one of Switzerland. Despite any affinities, the inhabitants of the Sundgau remain very attached to their own traditions. Half-timbered houses abound, most of which have rooftops with three faces because of the heavy winter snows. The countryside of gentle hills alternating between pastures and pond sprinkled woods contributes to the tranquil relaxing image of the region.

Altkirch, situated in the middle of the Sundgau, was for a long time the crossroads of southern Alsace, later to be replaced in this role by Mulhouse. The town's name reminds us of the old church that existed here until 1789 and that was a dependence of the Saint-Morand Priory. This same priory shelters the tomb of the evangelizing saint of the region.

The town was once dominated by a castle of the Counts of Ferrette, regional nobles. Because of the presence of this castle what had previously been a village was classed a town in 1215 and surrounded by a wall in 1330. Several years earlier Jeanne de Ferrette, last of her line, married the Archduke Albert II of Austria (known as Albert the Wise) bringing the region under control of the Hapsburgs. Catastrophes did not spare the region: the plague swept through in 1349, and an earthquake that brought the castle down shook this part of Alsace in 1356. The "Grande Bande" of Enguerrand de Coucy, profiting from the dark of night, tried in 1376 to storm the town. It was at this moment, however, that an "extraordinary light" shining down from the ramparts terrorized the attackers permitting the town residents to repell them. The town attributed this miracle to the Virgin Mary, and one still sees the statue erected in her honor

A house in Baldersheim

above the fountain in front of the town hall.

The fifteenth century was marked by war. Among the armed conflicts was the war with the Armagnacs who were allies of Charles the Bold. The war would end only in 1477 with the death of Charles near the city of Nancy. Altkirch's golden era came in the sixteenth century when the Bishop of Basel established his consistory here. In 1555 the Archduke of Austria granted the town control of and tax privileges on the sales of salt from Tyrolean mines. Authorization was also granted to construct a mill.

During the Thirty Years War the Swedish, the Imperial forces, and the French successively occupied Altkirch. Finally, in 1637 the Count of Grancey's troops burned the town. France annexed the region, and Louis XIV gave it to Cardinal Mazarin. After changing hands several times, the region eventually found itself a possession of the Grimaldi family of Monaco. During the eighteenth century Altkirch became a garrison city, and it was General Kléber who drew up the plans for the present day town hall. In 1857 the Basel-Mulhouse-Paris railroad line brought a noticeable economic upswing. Mulhouse had, however, already become the region's dominant industrial center.

Sundgau's countryside

A house in Heimsbrunn
A house in Biederthal

A beautiful bay-window in Landser
A house in Grentzingen

To the south of Altkirch, near Ferrette and above the little village of Levoncourt, stand the ruins of Morimont Castle. Rebuilt after the 1356 earthquake, the castle was destroyed in the middle of the fifteenth century toward the end of the conflict opposing the Hapsburgs and the Swiss confederates. The castle's owner Pierre de Morimont refused to be beaten and rebuilt the castle making it bigger than before. Today one may still view the vestiges of this veritable fortress, including one of its principal curiosities, the immense vaulted cellar.

Ferrette, with its two castles, was the key between the territories of the Hapsburgs and the Swiss Confederates. In 1633 the Sundgau peasants rebelled against rule by the Swedish mercenaries occupying the upper castle. The mercenaries massacred the rebels down to the very last man, forcing them to hang one another and then burning the castle.

Not far, the "Erdmannlefelsen" or dwarf grotto permits us to finish our tour of Alsace with a legend. A long time ago dwarves lived in the region of "Erdmannle", dwarves who worked for the inhabitants of the Sundgau on the condition that they never be seen. Curiosity prompted the women of the region to cover their floors with ashes one night so as to be able

to follow the tracks left by the dwarves the next day. The next morning the women broke out in laughter upon discovering from the prints left in the ashes that the dwarves were webfooted. The "Erdmannle", ashamed, fled to their grotto leaving the inhabitants of the Sundgau to do their own work ever since....

The castle of Morimont
The castle of Ferrette

INDEX

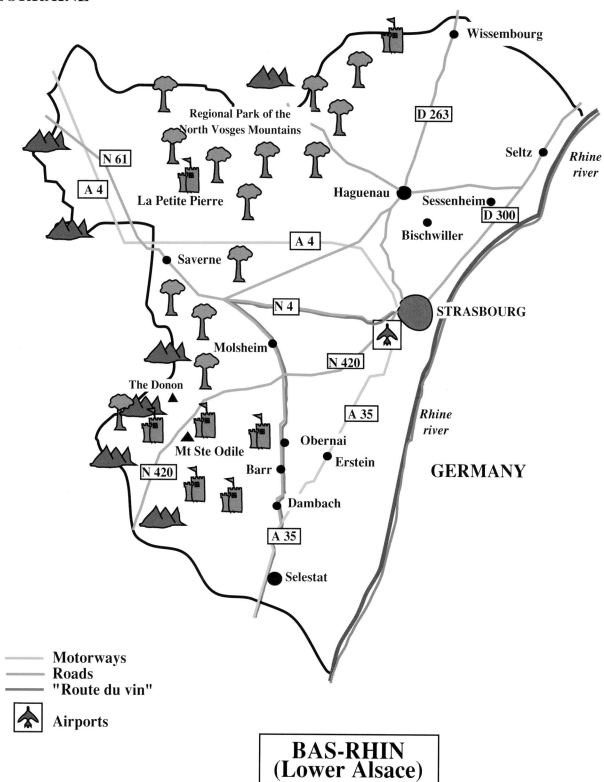

GERMANY

LORRAINE

Wissembourg

D 263

Regional Park of the
North Vosges Mountains

Seltz

Rhine river

N 61

A 4

La Petite Pierre

Haguenau

Sessenheim

D 300

Bischwiller

A 4

Saverne

N 4

STRASBOURG

Molsheim

N 420

The Donon

A 35

Rhine river

Mt Ste Odile

Obernai

GERMANY

N 420

Barr

Erstein

Dambach

A 35

Selestat

—— Motorways
—— Roads
—— "Route du vin"
✈ Airports

**BAS-RHIN
(Lower Alsace)**

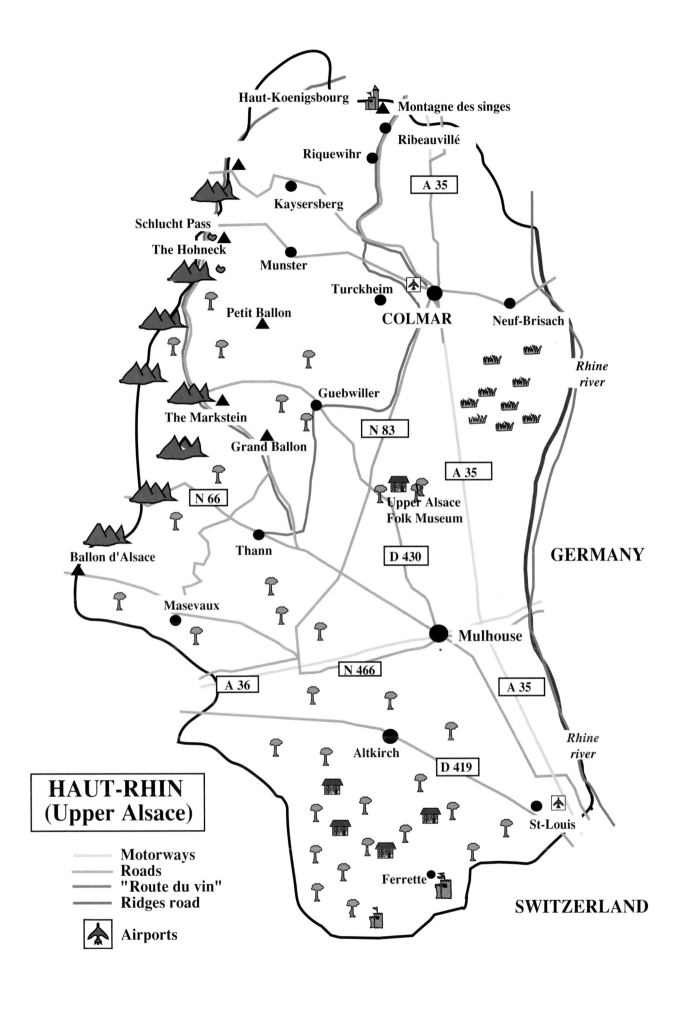

Haut-Koenigsbourg

Montagne des singes

Ribeauvillé

Riquewihr

A 35

Kaysersberg

Schlucht Pass

The Hohneck

Munster

Turckheim

COLMAR

Neuf-Brisach

Rhine river

Petit Ballon

Guebwiller

N 83

A 35

The Markstein

Grand Ballon

Upper Alsace Folk Museum

N 66

D 430

GERMANY

Ballon d'Alsace

Thann

Masevaux

Mulhouse

N 466

A 36

A 35

Altkirch

Rhine river

D 419

HAUT-RHIN
(Upper Alsace)

St-Louis

Ferrette

SWITZERLAND

Motorways
Roads
"Route du vin"
Ridges road
Airports

We would like to thank all those who allowed us to " wander through ALSACE", and especially:

M. Fleith from the Departemental Tourism Office of Bas-Rhin,

Mme Laurent from Departemental Tourism Association of Haut-Rhin,

M. Hofsess from the Regional Park of the North Vosges Mountains,

M. Renaud from the Center for the reintroduction of the storks in Hunawihr,

Mlle Merz from the " Montagne des singes ",

M. le Chanoine Diss from the Sainte-Odile Mount convent,

The European Council,

The Kronenbourg Brasserie,

Jacques Volcouve,

M. Gérard Becquet from the National Automobile Museum library,

Mme Löliger from Mulhouse's Tourism Office,

M. Lutz from Saverne's Tourism Office,

M. Rufra from Haguenau's Tourism Office,

and also Tourism Offices of Colmar, Guebwiller, Molsheim, Ribeauvillé,

Riquewihr, Sélestat, and Wissembourg,

who so kindly provided us with many pictures in this book,

and gave us so much information without which all of this would not have been possible.

Here are their addresses, and we strongly advise you to take contact them if you plan to visit this wonderful region.

Parc Naturel Régional des Vosges du Nord
Château - 67290 - La Petite Pierre
(Tél : 88 70 46 55)

Office Départemental du Tourisme du Bas-Rhin
Maison du Tourisme
9 rue du Dôme - 67000 Strasbourg
(Tél : 88 22 01 02)

Office du Tourisme de Colmar
4, rue d'Unterlinden - 68000 Colmar
(Tél : 89 41 02 29)

Office du Tourisme de Guebwiller
5, place Saint-Léger - 68500 Guebwiller
(Tél : 89 76 10 63)

Office du Tourisme de Haguenau
1, place Joseph-Thierry - 67500 Haguenau
(Tél : 88 73 30 41)

Syndicat d'initiative de Molsheim
Hôtel de ville - 67120 Molsheim
(Tél : 88 38 52 00)

Office du Tourisme de Mulhouse
9 avenue Foch - 68100 Mulhouse
(Tél : 89 45 68 31)

Office du Tourisme de Ribeauvillé
1 Grand-Rue - 68150 Ribeauvillé
(Tél : 89 73 62 22)

Office du Tourisme de Riquewihr
Place Voltaire - 68340 Riquewihr
(Tél : 89 47 80 80)

Office du Tourisme de Saverne
Grand-Rue - 67700 Saverne
(Tél : 88 91 80 47)

Office du Tourisme de Sélestat
Commanderie Saint-Jean
Boulevard du Général Leclerc
 - 67600 Sélestat
(Tél : 88 92 02 66)

Office du Tourisme de Wissembourg
Mairie - 67160 Wissembourg
(Tél : 88 94 10 11)

PHOTOS CREDITS :

Association Départementale du Tourisme du Haut-Rhin : pp.52 / 54 / 57 / 59

Brasserie Kronenbourg : p.29

Conseil de l'Europe : p.28

F. Gass (Office du Tourisme de Haguenau) : p.11

Hoerdt : pp.45 / 46

Löliger : pp.44 / 61 / 72 / 73 / 74 / 75 / 76 / 77 / 78 / 79 / 80 / 81 / 82 / 83 / 85 / 86 / 87 / 88-89 / 90 / 91 92 / 93

Lutz / Office du Tourisme de Saverne : p.13

J.F. Macaigne / P. Bastier : pp.11 / 13 / 21 / 24 / 25 32 / 33 / 35 / 50 / 51 / 53 / 55 / 56 / 57 / 60 / 62 / 63 65 / 71 / 78 / 81 / 82

Merz (Montagne des singes) : pp.42 / 43

Mont Sainte-Odile : p.31

Fleith / Office Départemental du Tourisme du Bas-Rhin : pp.3 / 6 / 7 / 9 / 11 / 12 / 13 / 14 / 21 / 23 / 24 / 25 / 26 / 27 / 30 / 34 / 35 / 36 / 41

Office du Tourisme de Colmar : p.57 / 58

Office du Tourisme de Guebwiller : pp.6 / 61 / 64 / 66 / 67 / 70 / 84

Office du Tourisme de Molsheim : p.35

Office du Tourisme de Riquewihr : pp.47 / 48-49 / 50 / 51

Office du Tourisme de Sélestat : p.37

Office du Tourisme de Wissembourg : pp.8 / 9 / 10 / 34

Parc Naturel Régional des Vosges du Nord : pp.15 / 16 / 17 / 18 / 19

J. Renaud : pp.4 / 5

S.I.V.O.M. / C.O.M. / Kempf : pp. 7 / 33 / 55 / 63 / 68-69

J. Volcouve : pp. 5 / 20 / 32

Volerie des aigles : p.42

Photos X : pp.21 / 22 / 38-39 / 40 / 41 / 62

Cover :   Eguisheim (Office du Tourisme de Guebwiller)

Back cover :   Andlau (O.D.T. du Haut-Rhin)

                                         Haut-Koenigsbourg (Photo X)

                                         Kammerzell house(J.F. Macaigne)

                                         Alsatian costume (O.D.T. du Haut-Rhin)

                                         Mulhouse National Automobile Museum (Löliger)

                                         Palace of Europe   (Conseil de l'Europe)

Inside front & back cover :   Cigognes du Centre de Réintroduction d'Hunawihr (J. Renaud)

Maps :   J.F. Macaigne

To be published, in the same collection:

Wandering through BRITTANY

Wandering through FRANCHE - COMTE

Wandering through LORRAINE

© TRAJECTOIRE COMMUNICATION - 1990
152 Avenue du Général Leclerc
54220 - MALZEVILLE
FRANCE

ISBN 2 - 908341 - 01 - 8

Wandering in ALSACE is also published
in french:
Promenades en ALSACE
ISBN 2 - 908341 - 00 - X
in german:
Spaziergang durch ELSASS
ISBN 2 - 908341 - 02 - 6

Achevé d'imprimer
en juin 1990
sur les presses de
VAGNER Imprimeur
Zone d'Activités Gabriel-Fauré
54140 Jarville-La Malgrange
Dépôt légal : 2e trimestre 1990